Women Writing:
On the Edge of Dark and Light

Women Writing:
On the Edge of Dark and Light

Edited by Kay Mullen

CATHERINE PLACE POETS

Copyright © 2015 by Catherine Place Poets

Published in the United States
by Pilgrim Spirit Communications, Tacoma, Washington.

All rights reserved. No part of this publication may be reproduced, distributed, or transmitted in any form or by any means, including photocopying, recording, or other electronic or mechanical methods, without the prior written permission of the publisher, except in the case of brief quotations embodied in critical reviews and certain other noncommercial uses permitted by copyright law.

ISBN-13: 978-0692455319
ISBN-10: 0692455310

Cover image by Rita H. Kowats
Book design by Judith Jones,
Pilgrim Spirit Communications

Acknowledgments

Special thanks to the Directors of Catherine Place, Judy Mladineo and Peg Murphy, OP, for their continued encouragement and support for the Catherine Place Poets, for all those who attended and promoted the yearly readings, and all who expressed an appreciation of poetry in so many ways.

Special thanks also to Rita Kowats for the cover photo: www.spiritualitywithoutborders.wordpress.com

and to Judith Jones, M.Div., publisher:
Pilgrim Spirit Communications (www.pilgrimspirit.com)

Acknowledgment is made to the following publications in which poems appeared previously, sometimes in slightly different form:

Sally McClintock
Wrist Magazine, "The Warm Spot"
Vermont Country Sampler, "My House"

Contents

Introduction ix

Nancy Taylor
      Perspective..11
      The Gardener 12
      Young and Unafraid 13
      Irony 14

Sherry Helmke
      Plains Huntress 15
      Erased Future..16
      The New Girl 17

Stephanie Ostmann
      Crossing the International Date Line ...18
      Drought 19
      Portrait of a Lady 21

Heidi Erdmann
      Teresita..23
      Do You Know 24
      A Different Flight....................................25
      Nighttime Rush 27

Sally McClintock
      The Warm Spot..28
      Hear Ye, Hear Ye......................................29
      My House 30

Martha Scoville
      Amtrak Rocks 31
      Kitchen Musing 33
      The Intruder...34
      Search Mode 35

Vonnie Cowan
- A Rush Through Iris 37
- Ritual 38
- Alchemy 39
- He Comes Home Singing 40

Carol Bohlman
- Old Love 41

Patty Kennedy
- Rewrite the Night 42
- Victory Chimes, Glory Be & Our Girl . 44
- On Seeing The Wind 46

Bev Fesharaki
- Blackberries 47
- Chocolate Stars 48
- Just Read It Honey 49
- Rt. 1, Sterling, Kansas 50

Pamela Reed
- The Illusionist 52
- Punica Granatum 53
- Answered Prayer 54

Glenna Cook
- So Many 56
- New Friend 57

Jonelle Soelling
- Moose 58
- How Did it Happen? 60
- Feathered Apes 62

Betty Karr
- Organics 64
- The Missing Muse 65

Contributors 67

Introduction

    Catherine Place in Tacoma is a space of healing, hope, and connection for all women and serves more than 1,470 women annually. The center was inspired by Catherine of Siena, a 14th century Dominican who worked to effect change in the society of her day. Catherine Place fosters community learning and growth, leadership, support, and empowerment.

    The Inscape poetry group of Catherine Place has been meeting for the past five years on a weekly basis with a yearly reading, and break from mid-July to October. The poets weave in and out for various reasons but an ongoing group continues to meet each week and all have discovered the power poetry continues to play in their lives. Each year one specific book on the writer's vocation is chosen for study and reflection. These have included: an anthology, *Cries of the Spirit: A Celebration of Women's Spirituality*, edited by Marilyn Sewell, works by Steve Kowit, Richard Hugo, Mary Oliver, and William Stafford.

    A highlight consists of weekly poet presentations of seasoned poets, a brief bio and several poems for consideration and discussion. Over one hundred poets have been presented from Rumi to modern day poets.

    To the question can writing be taught? Richard Hugo answers "yes and no it can't. Ultimately the most important things a poet will learn about writing are from (him) herself in the process."

    I am grateful for my own learning experiences as I share the good news of poetry with the gifted women whose poetry appears on the pages of this anthology.

Kay Mullen, MFA

Nancy Taylor

Perspective

When the Harvest Moon nods to winter,
spider webs hold my house hostage.
Aspen trees glitter gold
until leaves and temperatures drop.

While embracing autumn,
I dread winter when
incessant rain prompts me to consider
Prozac. My neighbor stops delivering
fresh eggs. His chickens don't like
this latitude at year's end either.

Winter has not besieged us yet
so I toss faded flowers into compost,
ready bird feeders, and cut a handful
of dahlias. The squirrels scurry
their treasure over the fence
and give me perspective.

Nancy Taylor

The Gardener

At first, my neighbor at the pea patch
was gruff. Perhaps establishing
a new garden was daunting or maybe
I resemble an ex. Taught to make
excuses for people, I don't give much
credence to first impressions.

Still, we toil side-by-side hands
in dirt. He with plan, notebook
and raised beds. I with shovel
of compost and foggy memory
of what may have worked years past.
After I remove a horseradish-infused
strawberry bed, replacing it with peppers,
he says, "peppers are better."
I should keep a notebook I tell myself
especially if the peppers do turn out better.

Harvest time, John's plot is dense
with veggies, mine half weeds.
He asks if I want to make pesto
offering an armful of basil and advises
how to kill critters making swiss cheese
out my leaves. He gives me spinach
seeds that grow well in our micro-climate
and encourages me to winter garden.

Now, when he glances sideways
I am reminded of my favorite brother.

Nancy Taylor

Young and Unafraid

The funeral doesn't unfold exactly
as the six-year-old planned.
He got the crypt so he wouldn't
be *stepped on* but not the mariachi
band he'd requested to lighten
heavy hearts. Only our memories
can do that.

I recall accessing his new
port the first time. Several nurses
entered the exam room to watch
the procedure, further frightening
an already terrified boy. As I pierce
his skin with stinging lidocaine,
his knee jerks and kicks me in the nose.
Stars circle like wind in a tornado
but I win the battle with blackout
and finish the task. Before the next
needle stick, this dying boy
begs his mother to hold his legs
so he can't kick me again.

Later, unafraid, he calmly tells me
"I am going to be with Jesus."

Nancy Taylor

Irony

I remember early morning hospital
rounds when I discover a patient whiter
than the sheet that covers her. The night
nurse fails to monitor vital signs or look
at the surgery site. She chooses not
to disturb the woman whose femoral artery
was bypassed the previous day.

I remember pulling back her covers to see
a pool of blood. I remember feeling
the patient's thready pulse and a strong
urge to choke the new grad nurse.
Instead, I summon the surgeon who panics
and pulls out the intravenous line dripping
heparin. "Now we don't have a line"
I yell before it occurs to me someone
needs to remain calm. I remember running
to the pharmacy to procure a heparin antidote
before carting a non-responsive patient back
to the OR.

I remember my ecstasy at seeing the woman
the following day and asking if she remembers
me. She says, "Your voice is familiar." I wonder
if she heard grace—or terror.

Sherry Helmke

Plains Huntress

A hungry marsh goddess peers along
the dusty river bank,
an imaginary plumb line linking long orange legs
to a slate blue crown.

Fierce irises
flaming like a prairie sunset's afterglow,
spy unsuspecting prey scooting belly-down
along the shallow bed.
The silvery fish's body shimmies only briefly
as the pointed beak breaks scales and skin.

Raindrops dot the thirsty earth
as mother heron aims
a second piercing spear.

Sherry Helmke

Erased Future

You knew
not to look back,
I knew
to stand at the glass
and watch your head not turn.
Hands deep in my robe pockets,
I listen as gravel
crunches beneath your feet,
retract my index finger
from the hilly topography
of what might have been.

Sherry Helmke

The New Girl

I do not know you
and yet I gather you,
by the elbow,
guide you to safety under the strong maple tree.
Your green dress, wrinkled and dirty,
hangs on your stunted frame.

A few days later
I notice how the dress
sprinkled with tiny amber flowers
glows in the sturdy tree's shadows
as playground taunts
splotch our six-year-old souls.

A sweet smile belies your untended body,
stubborn, greasy ringlets of hair
soften the hungry angles of your cheeks.
So quiet,
you never even said goodbye.

Stephanie Ostmann

Crossing the International Date Line

Sun rises in the west, streaks of rose
fade to gold on a blue eastward arc.

Shopkeepers unbundle purchases.
Commuters shift cars into reverse.
Radio voices undo today's revelations
and horrors.
Cows amble backward
to the dim barn from sunny pastures.
Coffee flows upward, steaming drip
cools to clear water.

Lovers uncouple
their embraces, bedsprings
rise softly
Night-blooming flowers fold
their petals, inhaling
fragrant sighs.
Sour breath sweetens.

This flight will arrive yesterday.

If I make this journey three hundred times
will you be there to greet me
at the start
wearing your warm mortal flesh
bearing a goodbye kiss
speaking your plans for tomorrow?

Stephanie Ostmann

Drought

You never were a waterfall,
laughing, singing
sprouting wildflowers from your brow
catching sunlight in your mist
changing course from year to year.

No,
your water still
and deep,
I always knew where to find you,
watched you
reflect the sky and lap the shore.
You watered my roots deeply,
making not delight but assurance.
I never doubted your love.

Once we stood beside a lake
father, daughter,
watched evening roll in streaks across the water.
My nine-year-old arms around your waist
I asked
how old are you? Your answer
chilled my arithmetic in mid-air.
Your life half gone,
I could not bear to loose my hold.

Now we stand far beyond that sum.
Life's long, slow arc has parched you,
receded your waters,
surfacing stubble and weary worn stones.
Contours of shore that shaped your life
have shifted, altered the rhythmic lapping of your days.
You can no longer touch what made you whole.

Stephanie Ostmann

My arms recall the comfort of your once waist
now a fragile armature wearing skin like paper.
Watching from the shore
I am powerless.
I cannot bring you rain.

Stephanie Ostmann

Portrait of a Lady

She'd wear spandex without apology
    leopard-spotted or flamingo pink
    clinging to her ample thighs
    striking the eye with glare
    even on an overcast day.
She'd keep her nails long
    curved like a mandarin's
    never a one broken
    lacquered metallic green or lilac
    embellished with delicate flowers
    and perhaps a touch of glitter.
She'd wear rings, one or two too many,
    purchased on QVC
    for an unbelievably low price.
    She'd watch *Real Housewives of Atlanta*
    hold all the crumpled facts
    on Fox News as Truth.
She'd leave a path of footprints on the carpet
    treading back and forth
    from sofa to refrigerator door
    to retrieve yet another Diet Pepsi.
She'd sit on the back stoop chain-smoking
    glaring at lesser creatures who slink by
    relieving her boredom
    by shedding thoughts like loosened fur
    in muttered catty comments
    and warnings: "Never forget this place is *mine*."
She would if she were human.

As it is she must content herself
with leaving tufts of grey and white
on the coverlet
twitching her tail in disdain

Stephanie Ostmann

hissing at her long-haired housemate
and occasionally drawing blood
from the hand that feeds her.

Heidi Erdmann

Teresita

Ladino smile, blue jeans,
cross imbedded on a silver belt buckle
reveals four corners and a sturdy stance
rooted in Mayan spirituality.
Solidarity ring replaces a wedding band
to form a new celibacy of faithfulness,
to the Corn People.
Indigo beads belie a sensuous femininity,
dimples give way to a youthful spunkiness,
no evidence of her broken spirit
healed by an ancestral talk.

Untangling an identity of hiding in privilege
or walking with risk,
she listens to a call given at birth for justice.
Stones cry out to tell the Mayan Priests her truth
without justifications.
She is side-tracked by her compañeros
whose deaths thunder through the mountains
of Guatemala.
When faced with clay jars
filled with bones of the massacred,
she is seized and shakes with love.
God sprouts again through her grief,
as maize grows between lava stones.

Hope balances with despair,
martyrdom brings resurrection,
breakdown leads to new conviction,
fear buried far away.
She finds her way home,
an unquestionable love
for the indigenous poor.

Heidi Erdmann

Do You Know

I have a feminine smile
My dog is a princess
No piercing or tattoos
so I can hide as a straight edge

And you will not know
I have sucked up the headlines

Hesitate before I hug a child
so you cannot say I am a pervert

Back away when I see an infant
so you can keep me from adopting

Look away when two women touch
so you don't realize I feel exposed

Pause when I put my arm around my partner
so you don't feel uncomfortable

Cringe when you touch me
so you don't suspect I like it

Blush when you smile at me
so you don't think I am leering

Pretend I don't feel anything
so you can't hurt me anymore

Heidi Erdmann

A Different Flight

She builds the nest
but never lays the eggs.
Doesn't count toes
or wipe a bottom.
Never reads bedtime stories
or puts on a band aid.
No sleep-overs, birthday cakes,
extra loads of laundry,
or homework hassles.
She's spared the pouty face,
the rolling eyes,
never has to say
"No! And I mean it!"
watch the clock late at night,
listen for the door,
hear " I love you, Mom."
or sees her own reflection
in someone else's eyes.
No showers, weddings,
in-laws to meet.
No grand kids to baby-sit,
pictures to show off.
She never has an empty nest,
never fills it.
Her flight
takes a different course.

She flies over oceans,
studies others' nests,
marches for nest equality,
gives hope for those kicked out.
Forms new nest communities,
creates safe nests for fledglings,

Heidi Erdmann

some with broken nests,
guides those eager to fly.
She evolves the consciousness
of nest builders.
With room to move,
she creates a new flight plan.

Heidi Erdmann

Nighttime Rush

Almost every morning the plane leaves
before my bags are packed.
I'm still folding my sleep
when the alarm goes off.
Piles of problems reproduce
faster than I can collect my thoughts.
Zippers break as I roll over.
I try to scream while grabbing for handles.
The thought of leaving stuff never occurs to me.
I hear "The cabin doors are closing"
and wake in a hot sweat
frustrated I missed another flight
because my baggage got in the way again.

Sally McClintock

The Warm Spot

The phone call. "Mother died."
I rush up the hill to my mother's bedside,
stand beside her cooling body.

I close her jaw. It falls open.
I close it again
and discover a warm spot on her neck,
a spot of lingering heat,
a mother-spot that winter has not reached.

I ponder how she made me
out of this body
which has just died,
yet her neck still warm

and I have found it,
and felt it,
and my spirit lightens.

Sally McClintock

Hear Ye, Hear Ye

Brothers and sisters,
Daughters and grandmothers,
Hear me.
No more of your songs.
The village does not need your music.
Politicians are coming.
Ring the bells, start the drumming.
Artists, muffle your colors.

Sally McClintock

My House

As I struggle up the steps with my groceries,
Alyce comes by with her little dog and offers help.
I say I don't want her to see the house, it's the messiest yet
but she says, "Listen, I was a home health nurse
and I've seen *everything*. This is your home
and you can do anything you want with it."
So in she goes with my groceries,
past the dining table covered with papers and projects,
past the kitchen table with stacks of paper, marking pens,
scissors, box of stamps, stapler,
right up to the messy counter where she sets the bags down.
I forgot to mention the two sinks of dirty dishes,
the floor with bits of food, traces of oat bran cereal,
nut crumbs, raisins, blueberries--
Why sweep it up? There'll just be more. And
Alyce says it's *my* house.

Martha Scoville

Amtrak Rocks

Past forests filled with witness trees
limbs reach to tell stories
of what was seen in 1863
when brothers' blood flowed freely
about their gnarled roots.

Past farmhouses where families gather
nightly at early supper
to forge their joys and sorrows
into familiar fables.

Past floodplains flat and riverbound
flocked with puddle ducks
dabbling and upending
to feed on marsh grasses
and hovering flies.

Past factories fuming with production
unapologetic grey hulks
shouldering their way
into land, air space, and waterway
insistent engines of industry.

Past frontiers of Cowboys, Rodeos,
First Nation peoples
redolent with sagebrush,
pungent leather, drumming hoofbeats.

Past the New Frontier challenging us,
the anointed,
to change a world we knew,
believing it was possible.

Martha Scoville

And now forward to the final frontier,
these window-captured photos,
a stitched-together fabric
of history and perception,
a laprobe to finger
while that world so quickly slips away.

Martha Scoville

Kitchen Musing

maybe eternity starts
      watching pasta boil

maybe hesitant hands entwine
      suspending time

maybe cosmic clashes
      strike us mid-sentence

maybe stars align
      though clouds obscure sight

maybe celestial circumstance
      changes our course

maybe star-pierced firmament
      splinters an obsidian sky

maybe shattered light
      splashes a kitchen floor

a melange of moonlight and fettuccine

Martha Scoville

The Intruder

He visits me at importune moments.
A rude visitor with no sense of decorum.
How can he walk in the front door
without knocking?
Why not call ahead to let me know
he's coming?
Even a text, however impersonal
could conciliate me.
What right does he have
to assume my warm welcome?

A few years ago I spent a lot of time with him,
thought he was interesting company.
Together we explored some of the darkest
places I had ever been.
It was our secret
we kept it from everyone.

But then it went too far.
I couldn't commit only to him.
I packed up all his stuff that lay around my house
the Roy Orbison CDs, the pills, the self-help books,
buried them in the front yard
near the boulder covered with ivy.

I thought we were done.
It was over.

Recently I spotted him lurking in the neighborhood.
I pretend I don't see him.
But I know *Grief* is there, in the shade — waiting.

Martha Scoville

Search Mode

I shouldn't but I do.
Google an old boyfriend on the web.
He lives in Sun City now.
Even today, when passing a pale green
'72 Volvo sedan, I'm sure it's him with me
sitting beside him glancing down
floor mats stenciled with his parents' names
Martin, on the driver's side
Margaret, the passenger.

There's a photo in the Sun City Independent
January 2013 issue
tall, in the back row, a bit stooped
flanked by seven women in floral prints.
Not his type.
He preferred younger women
with some style.

A caption extolls these eight
newly trained literacy tutors, him
"distinguished and successful"
agency director serving troubled youth.
I never knew why he was suspended.
Must have been money or ethics,
easily both.

Leaning into the computer screen
I squint to pull pixels together
to form that familiar quirk in his smile.
Grainy dots punctuate a flat grey orb.
It could be anybody.

Martha Scoville

Details distilled or deleted
his Facebook profile of comfort
and convenience ends
with a mouse click.

Arizona – who would have thought?

Vonnie Cowan

A Rush Through Iris

The trillium bulbs
turn under the earth,
cherry trees flock with blossoms.
A song sparrow sends
a note to a robin high on a branch.

I'm listening for a song, a crying
sound, an osprey learning to fly.

My voice still, afraid, the defense
of my soul hidden somewhere,
somewhere I've known yet
not remembered, a rush through iris
that leaves only essence.

Vonnie Cowan

Ritual

I always earn money
doing the laundry.
There at the bottom
of the white machine,
soaking wet heavy sheets,
one lonely sock, sweaters
in knots, jeans with Kleenex
in the pocket, all waiting
for me. I untie the troubled
sweaters, the sheets
bound together like lovers.
The bother, to haul one
drenched bunch from one
white machine to another.
The first thing to do,
clean the filter always
full of grey gritty balls
of lint. Reloading the machine
for the next ritual, I find
at the bottom
one very wet dime.

Alchemy

She told me from the beginning,
 "You need a name
for your business, Mother."
I laughed and said, "If folks
want me, they'll find me."

After she died, I remembered
her magic, the chemistry
she had with children
and animals, the love she gave
her elixir of life,
her soul and spirit full of alchemy.

She is with me now.
When I work, she whispers
colors. Furniture moves itself.
I hear her say, "Alchemist, Mother."
I bow and say "yes."

Vonnie Cowan

He Comes Home Singing

I know his heart's with her.
Though warm and loving
he lies next to me, he sleeps
better cradled in her arms.

In the new white flowing dress
he bought her, she spirits him
away, whispers softly, wind
and water lapping his heart.

He comes home singing.
She knows how to woo him
properly, shine his spirit,
blood of his being
wild song of his soul.

He puts her to sleep
with gentle care, folds
her gown, pats here and there,
murmurs of their next meeting,
his mistress,

Sailboat

Carol Bohlman

Old Love

They sit together
at the dining table
oblivious to others.

He whispers cherished words,
the only sound, her soft laugh.
Like a raspberry colored rose,
her cheeks bloom a pink blush
as they celebrate another anniversary.

With effort, the elderly couple
exits the restaurant.
With halting steps, he unlocks the car
for his fragile wife
who waits patiently with her cane.

The sky blue
as just washed café crockery,
the sun smiles overhead.
She squints, the laugh lines
furrow deeply in her face.

Radiant
she adores him with her gaze.
He holds her tightly.
Sixty years
seems only yesterday.

Patty Kennedy

Rewrite the Night
"While pensive poets painful vigils keep"
          Alexander Pope

I need a dark and pensive mood
   to love the night
or else some long
and hard-edged drinking
kind of tight
          reminds me
          of those long gone
          party times of mine
the midnight years
when we could change the world
we'd mock the faux
and read the fictional account.

In evening dreams our velvet gowns
and colored pearls
          the city's soft
          and smooth
          *illuminated nigh*t
perpetuate the time
with nothing
but a word.
It takes a dark and pensive mood
   to love the night.

These finely darkened shadows
long to break the light
          endure the last
          and empty hours
          that write each day
we'll dress for dinner
see a spotlight show sublime.

Patty Kennedy

Or make new plans
we'll speak our purred regrets
      so *pour us*
      wine and light
      your cigarette
It takes a dark and pensive mood
  to love the night.

Patty Kennedy

Victory Chimes, Glory Be & Our Girl
a tale of sister ships

Victory Chimes
      her bell and horn
  men cheer and yell across the harbor.

Two brooms out
lashed high to the rail
  in pride and relief.
They've swept the water
  twice
  and sold twice
one hundred thousand fish.
We'll all be rich.

Glory Be
   sings the Father
    and His Manly Son
       and the Great Holy Spirit
swimming alongside
our salmon
seiners seining
diesel fuel
salt
and the muddy stench of seagull shallows
low tides left behind.

Our Girl
   rushes to the run
that's coming and come
and may not long
  be here among us.

Our Girl allied with *Glory* and *Victory*
her brother, her son.

Patty Kennedy

   Amen they say.
   Amen and the women
know chill uncharted bays
souls far below their depths
pure intention filling their prayers
their orisons and intercessions.
Grace here
   among us
to save us from our fears.

Flags sail the breezes
blowing hard from big seas
calling men to their own:
   their wealth, their debts
   their sudden death.

Bless'ed are we who come
in the name of the Father
content as a deck cat
when the boats return full
   of sockeye and pinks
   silvers and kings.

Jesus, Mary, Joseph
   keep us
   and thanks be
to God the All
Good and Deserving
for these fine fish
   our living harvest
   our ocean benediction.

Victory Chimes with *Glory Be*
as *Our Girl* rushes
to fish the swiftly turning tide.

Patty Kennedy

On Seeing The Wind

    outside
the maple branch waves
again, stranded
    on this winded bluff
roots arbored in the quiet dust above
the silent little bay
    gray leaden now
bright white before

 bright white
the salted waters wave
rise and break with silvered edge
gusting free in the last brief rays
of a long lightened day

 still muddy clouds
    so full of rain
call on the far horizon line
past the big bay
    where Fair Harbor lies
the distant trees
reach out the same way
    they lean to the wind
and they wildly wave

      and they wave
as my tethered maple waves
a welcome nod in forced repose
    they grapple
and spar with the brisk
new breeze bringing rain
    on the hint
    of an incoming tide
and ringing
    my hanging Chinese chimes.

Bev Fesharaki

Blackberries

Grandmother parks the car
at the edge of the dusty alley.
We walk, buckets in hand, to find
treasure among the sticker bushes.

Grandmother says the snakes will stay away
if we keep talking so, we do, ignoring
scratched arms, purple fingers, itchy noses.
As berries thump the bucket's bottom
we gather secrets and share them
to scare the snakes away.

Back home berries bob in cold water.
Hands, gnarled and new
rinse dust from the black orbs.
At the narrow counter we
roll dough and sprinkle sugar.

While pies bubble in the oven,
my fresh scratches crust over,
satisfied to be soothed
by Grandmother's white-hot wisdom
and warm blackberry pie.

Bev Fesharaki

Chocolate Stars

On Saturday mornings, while mom works,
Daddy rummages through the tool department at Sears
in search of just the right wrench, washer, hammer.
Then we ride the narrow escalator

down to the first floor where the chocolate stars
snuggle behind clear glass, between the malt balls
and vanilla fudge. I try to risk, to choose white
or beige, but the familiar stars soon rest
on my tongue. The ridges go first,
deliciously, gradually, gone. Top and bottom
both smooth, I know the star is fading.

There are more stars in the crisp white bag
but Daddy's calloused hand takes mine, soft,
trusting. I won't pull away to reach for more stars.
Instead I hold his touch, sweeter than chocolate
and more fleeting as it fades.

Bev Fesharaki

Just Read It Honey

Don't change adjectives to fit the mood,
don't read the setting more glamorous,
the weather more sunny.
Read it as written with coffee mug stains,
chipped fingernails and smeared lipstick.
Read your truth, not a slanted story.
It's too late to change your blues to yellow,
your weeds to roses.
Hummingbirds may replace crows, but later.

Just Read It Honey

Lives tend toward dangling participles,
subjects and verbs rarely agree, antecedents
go missing while adverbs ache.
No fair reaching into your fragile bag of lovely language,
because now's too late for shoulda, woulda, coulda.
What if and if only won't work here.
Cracking voice, shaky hands begging for approval,
as vulnerable as an infant, as ready to learn,

Just Read It Honey

Bev Fesharaki

Rt. 1, Sterling, Kansas

Dad's childhood home,
the whitewashed farmhouse
with the mailbox on a post out front.

Grandmother fetched my letters from that mailbox.
I wrote of my friends, school, books.
When she wrote she told the weather,
the cold, crisp winter mornings,
the dry spell, the far field, the back forty.

August took us back to help with the harvest.
Expansive fields of winter wheat, too heavy
for granddad to lift without sons, so we drove,
me resting in the back window of the Oldsmobile.

I'd seen pictures of Daddy's home,
weathered white behind him. His overalls
too small, hair combed slick, a ten year
old grin, squinting in the sun.
I'd seen pictures but didn't know
how worn the plank stairs,
how wide the porch,
how far the nearest tree.

The green frame of the screen door slams
as grandmother wipes her hands on her apron,
prepares for her son's embrace. He lifts her.
Her tired feet in sturdy shoes swing
for the first time in months.

Bev Fesharaki

He lifts her and she glows,
his grown up grin still wide,
thinning hair still slicked,
eyes still squinting in the sun,
he lifts her as
    his memory still lifts me.

Pamela Reed

The Illusionist

He saunters across playgrounds,
fields approving smiles along
with the sudden return of a ball
accompanied by blackslaps, wisecracks
and never ending nicknames
that pick me up and carry me
out of the mere ordinary
into the embrace of his spirit.

Steps taken two at a time
with a buoyancy orcas would envy.
His cassock doesn't sway. It strains
like me, to remain in his wake,
within his shadow, on the edge of his gaze,
in the grasp of his laughter.

"We're so lucky to have him."
"Could have been sent anywhere."
"What a blessing." "What?"
"A blessing—
to share this Sunday supper with him."

Heads bow over scalloped potatoes
and bowls of innocence.
Mother's maiden manners revisit
and coax girl grace back into full bloom
while sincerity is served
to the unsuspecting.

Pamela Reed

Punica Granatum

I reach in and scoop
your moist eagerness
only to watch you
glisten across my palm,
slip between my arthritic fingers
and cascade down the drain,
along with a shower of half filled memories.

Will I ever regain
that long-ago love?
Will I ever reclaim
the taste of your touch?

Probably not.

My yearning to have what once was,
surely not the intention
of this untouched pomegranate.

Pamela Reed

Answered Prayer

You came to her, emerged from the darkened stall
with barely a name, even less, an owner.
She whispered you into the light,
coaxed, cajoled, corralled your confidence.

She dined you with timothy hay, shirt-shined apples,
bent to dig stones from your hooves,
surprised you with midnight visitations
feathered you into your own.

On the dirt, as often as your back,
bruises and sprains waved away.
This twinned education inviting excellence,
schooled by patience and everlasting promise.

In uniform, she presents you:
bathed, brushed, conditioned,
enters the ring under the judge's watchful gaze
and cooler competition.

"Ladies and gentlemen, Lily Smolan
riding Answered Prayer."
Silence
       Then

The two of you
       Breathing as one
       Blasting around corners
       Barnstorming bliss

Pamela Reed

The two of you
>   Screaming over fences
>   Ears forward, full focus, flying

*Past fault, past fear, into a future
none of us could ever have imagined.*

Glenna Cook

So Many

So many days behind me,
    making more valuable
        those which remain.
So many seeds squandered,
    thrown where only sorrows grow,
        wrested in desolate darkness.
So many grown in fertile soil,
    fostering a tangled garden
        of abundance.
So many things lost: children's
    young years slipping through my arms
        as in a dream.
So many braver colors
    I could have used to paint my past,
        finer wines to fill my glass.
So many ways I now reach out
    to grasp each new day's offerings
        as gift and recompense for loss.

Glenna Cook

New Friend

Here at the art museum,
two hours spent filling my eyes with imagery,
I become aware of your insistent presence.
My right hand,
resting in the crook of my left arm,
begins to tremble. My gait
betrays a slight unsteadiness.
For now I shall call you P.
Soon I'll be ready to say your full name.

I have decided to love you, a part of me
I didn't ask for, but won't reject,
now that I know you're not leaving.

You even serve a purpose, sending me
places I may otherwise be too lazy to go,
if I didn't feel your tug. Last week,
I walked along Ruston Way, felt the cool
breeze coming off the water on a hot afternoon.
Wednesday, I met a friend for lunch.
Today, I'm here.

You'll be my incentive
to fill my days with nourishing pursuits,
reminding me that each moment I'm alive
I can choose to be grateful.

Jonelle Soelling

Moose

The French would call him a debrouillard.
The law firm next door keeps his green
food dish heaped. An unseen patron leaves
opened cans of cat food for him on the sidewalk.
He sprints three flights to my apartment
for beef and chicken treats,
never salmon, which he doesn't like.
Afterwards he drinks from the toilet bowl.

He has a home with food and flea medicine.
To say he has an owner would not be accurate.
He owns us.
When he visits me, he opens kitchen cabinets
with his right paw.
I open closet doors for him, curious
about his curiosity.

Scents command his attention.
He marks and re-marks the stove, refrigerator,
desk, reading chair.
He patrols an entire city block, front and back,
marking bushes, license plates, fences, gates.
He runs off challengers in all night vigils.

The two of us have a language now. Looks, chirps,
choice of rug, the sound of the front door.
When I am absorbed in piano practice, he slowly
walks around the piano, then under it,
signaling gently that he wants to go out.

I wash my clothes when I see how he cares
for his one black suit.

Jonelle Soelling

When he wants attention, he holds his tail
like an antenna and trolls the sidewalk.
Sometimes he sprawls on my desk asleep.
I see his body rise and fall.
He creates a pool of stillness.
I become quiet from the gift of his calm.

Jonelle Soelling

How Did it Happen?

We began as colleagues
on expense account, traveling on planes,
eating the best food.
I was engaged to a scientist who studied malaria.
He was married with two young children,
a wife who was correctly suspicious.

A justice of the peace eventually married us
in a small backyard ceremony, his children absent.
I chose an emerald green business suit, and
wore it to the office afterwards.

What had brought us together was his craving
to coach someone, to have his imprint on another.
This fit my desire to perfect myself.
I practiced the piano while
he did the cooking, even bread-making.
We had long conversations over dinner.

Thirty years later we were half-way through
a six-month stay in Mexico.
Each of us studied Spanish at the same school.
His tutor made flash cards with hand drawn pictures
of vegetables.
She lent him a Mexican cookbook.

Can you know something and not know it
at the same time?

He invited her to coffee without me on a Saturday.
They discussed her cupcake business,
stalled banking career and failed marriage.
She introduced him to friends from Mexico City.

Jonelle Soelling

He began going to the gym and losing weight.
Friends reported seeing them together
at cafes around town.

The day arrived when she invited both of us
to her home. The two of them cooked together,
huddled close like they did in Spanish class.
While her young son and I watched with curiosity,
they carried on like lovers.

The next morning, in the company of calla lilies,
I made a plan.
I would increase my hours at the Mayan Book
Cooperative, commit myself to writing in Spanish, and
join an art therapy group where I could paint.

I would prepare.

After lunch in the garden two days later,
he announced the end of our marriage.
No discussion. No mention of her.
"I should have done it sooner," he said.

People always ask two questions: how long were you
married, and did you have any warning, any clues.

I always say no.

Jonelle Soelling

Feathered Apes

My father, ninety two, knows that crows
recognize human faces.
He also accepts they hold funerals.

Sometimes crows bestow gifts on those
who feed them every day.
A yellow bead, blue paper clip, small metal
butterfly.

Today's conversation with my father meanders
to what we know about crows, their different
warnings for cats, hawks, and humans,
their ability to make complex tools, previously
attributed only to elephants and chimpanzees.

I told my father about the man
who asked crows he was feeding why they
never gave him anything.
The next day a worn red candy heart
with the word love
appeared in the middle of the feeding tray.

"That's preposterous," he said. "Crows can't
understand language."
"What about body language?" I countered.
"Like dogs and wolves. Those crows
understood."

Silence was his response, our closeness
slipping away.

"A young girl received a pearl-colored heart
for giving crows peanuts every day,"

Jonelle Soelling

I persisted.
"I'll refrain from commenting," he said.

"Caw caw caw," I answered,
my own call of distress.

Betty Karr

Organics

The trouble with eating healthy:
missing the pot lucks
and no one to commiserate
about the aging maladies
and health issues we share.

The trouble with thinking healthy
encourages thoughts
of living in a sterile environment
like a bubble—someplace
where pure oxygen is breathed.

The trouble with remaining healthy:
finding a non-toxic location
away from all life forms
including runaway bacteria
and viruses.

The trouble with optimal health,
the disturbing question
How will I ever die?
Will I eventually have to overdose
on sugar and gluten?

Mostly, good health fills me
with longing to consume
the bottle of Napa Valley Cabernet
waiting in the wine rack

along with the dark chocolate
and organic goat cheese hidden
in the back of the fridge
while viewing
Heart Health on PBS.

The Missing Muse

When I have fears
and fade off to sleep
everything erupts
in a dream.

I am lost at sea
moving upstream
on the edge of anxiety
seeking relief from fear.

The missing muse
not found in the usual places:
libraries, nature walks, solitude,
or the tiny hippy coffee shop.
Not there.

A champ of optimism,
there will be a poem
when least expected,
things take the time they take.
Don't worry.

It's enough to know that some
people always come through.
I'm ready for a poem
but it hasn't arrived.

Not yet.

CONTRIBUTORS

Carol Bohlman grew up in New Jersey. She is a retired teacher and addictions counselor with a focus on women's issues. She has facilitated women's self-esteem groups, worked as a chaplain's assistant, and currently volunteers at Catherine Place. Carol enjoys reading, gardening, traveling and sharing time with her adult children and seven grandchildren. She and her husband live in Steilacoom, Washington.

Glenna Cook is a wife, grandmother, great grandmother and poet and is a native of the Pacific Northwest. She graduated from the University of Puget Sound with a degree in English Literature. She has been published in a variety of journals, including *Raven Chronicles*, *Spiritdrift*, *Quill and Parchment*, and *Avalon Review*. She is an Alum of Hedgebrook, a writer's retreat for women on Whidbey Island.

Vonnie Cowan is a design consultant. She studied gardens, tea ceremony, and Ikebana in Japan. She taught design in Tokyo and Oizumi. Her interests are gardens and making jewelry. She lives with her husband, Bill, in Fircrest, Washington.

Heidi Erdmann is a school counselor, world traveler, and social justice promoter. She is most passionate about church reform, LGBT equality and positive behavior supports for youth in our schools. She lives in Tacoma with her wife, Kathleen, of 32 years and their Maltese dog, Gracie.

Contributors

Bev Fesharaki has taught writing to elementary students and served as an instructional facilitator, mentor, presenter and literacy coach for teachers. Her work has been published in *Wrist Magazine* and on the *MONA* website. She is a reader, golfer, grandmother and friend, and recently moved to Mukilteo where she continues writing, takes Zumba classes and contemplates her new view.

Sherry Helmke is an "accidental" poet. She has discovered new ranges of her voice by writing poetry. Innovation fascinates her and she works with individuals and teams to spark discoveries and breakthroughs. Nebraska-born, she now lives within walking distance of the Lake Michigan shore following sojourns in the Pacific Northwest and India.

Betty Karr has been a business owner for twenty-nine years managing publishers and authors, physicians, and legislators for major conferences and book tours. She is a convener for the Millionth Circle Initiative, member of Gather the Women Global Matrix, Fifth World Conference for Women and Toast Masters International. She is an advocate for the rights of women and children, and resides in Tacoma, Washington.

Patty Kennedy has published poems in online journals and regional anthologies with encouragement from the Pot Luck Poets of Gig Harbor, Inscape Poets of Tacoma, and other friends. She started the Gig Harbor Library's Poetry Reading Series in 2007 and continues to sponsor their spring and fall reading and writing workshops.

Contributors

Sally McClintock has worked for social justice and human rights as a community organizer, investigative journalist, and peace activist. She turned to poetry to address the human condition in a different way. Her writings appear in *Wrist Magazine*, *Vermont Country Sampler*, *Liberal Opinion Week*, and *Senior Scene*. She lives in Tacoma.

Stephanie Ostmann has been an artist working in paper and fabric. She taught art to students at elementary, secondary, and college levels and communication skills to adults. She is a certified mediator, a reading tutor and an outdoor enthusiast enjoying gardening, hiking, bicycling and skiing. Born in Portland, Oregon, she currently lives in Fircrest, Washington.

Pamela Reed was born in Tacoma and has made her living as an actor in New York and Los Angeles for the last forty years. She now divides her time between Tacoma and Los Angeles and is delighted to be a member of the Catherine Place poets. She is married to Sandy Smolan. They have two children, Reed and Lily.

Martha Scoville was born in Nebraska, spent her early years on the east coast and now lives in the Northwest. After many years teaching early childhood education, she served as consultant to regional and national programs to strengthen families and eliminate poverty. She is a naturalist and citizen scientist who studies plants and animals and their habitats. She enjoys kayaking, hiking, reading, and traveling.

Contributors

Jonelle Soelling is a classical pianist, visual artist, and writer. She has been artist in residence at the Belmont Hill School in Boston and the Vermont Studio Center in Johnson, Vermont. She has written about her exploration of jazz and recorded *One Step Closer*, a CD of both classical and jazz compositions for solo piano. She enjoys hiking and biking, and lives in the Pacific Northwest.

Nancy Taylor is a retired nurse practitioner who spent thirty years in a wide variety of nursing positions. She cared for pediatric oncology patients, and was an elementary school nurse for a DOD school at a US navy base in Japan. As a nurse she worked at an HMO and Mary Bridge Children's Hospital in the endocrine clinic with diabetic children. Nancy enjoys walking her two dogs, gardening, reading, and the symphony.

www.ingramcontent.com/pod-product-compliance
Lightning Source LLC
Chambersburg PA
CBHW060426050426
42449CB00009B/2152